A PUFF OF SMOKE

By the same author
Emer's Ghost
(Antelope)
The Finn Gang

A PUFF OF SMOKE

Catherine Sefton

Illustrated by Thelma Lambert

HAMISH HAMILTON LONDON

A book for
Tom Cosgrave

First published in Great Britain 1982
by Hamish Hamilton Children's Books
Garden House 57–59 Long Acre London WC2E 9JZ

British Library Cataloguing in Publication Data
Sefton, Catherine
A puff of smoke. – (Gazelle books).
I. Title II. Lambert, Thelma
823'.914 [J] PZ7

ISBN 0-241-10707-5

Filmset in 'Monophoto' Baskerville
by Eta Services (Typesetters) Ltd, Beccles, Suffolk
Printed in Great Britain by Fakenham Press, Ltd,
Fakenham, Norfolk

Chapter One

Beaky Kelly came down to breakfast, feeling bored. He ate his cornflakes, feeling bored, and then he started to pack his school-bag, feeling bored.

"I wish something would *happen*!" he said.

And something did.

There was a whirry noise in the kitchen, like a clockwork motor running down.

"What's that?" Beaky muttered, looking round him and wondering if the food mixer had gone mad again.

It wasn't the food mixer, and it wasn't the fridge, and it wasn't the canary being sick. He was still wondering what it could be when he smelt something odd, like . . . like . . .

"Mum!" Beaky called. "Mum! Something's burning!"

CRAAACKLEFFIILLLZZZ!

There was a blue, blinding flash, followed by a crackling sound, and

CORN

Beaky found himself whirled across the kitchen, so that he ended up on the floor beside the fridge. The canary's cage was swinging wildly to and fro, and the cat's milk was spilt.

"I . . . I . . ." Beaky gasped. "MUM! MUM! I've been blown up!"

But he hadn't been blown up. He was all right.

Something was sitting on the table, glowing.

It was a small red box, and its glow cast a red light on the corn-flakes packet and the milk jug.

Beaky had no idea where it had come from, but he knew it hadn't been there when he was eating his cornflakes. It was about the size of a matchbox, and on the side facing Beaky was written:

OTHER SIDE UP

Beaky picked up the box, to turn it over.

"Ouch!"

The box was red hot, and hurt his fingers, but the odd thing was that it didn't burn the plastic table top when Beaky dropped it.

The red box sat on the table, still glowing.

"Mum!" Beaky called, not wanting to go near it again.

Mrs Kelly didn't come. She was trying to get Mr Kelly out of bed in time for work. Getting Dad up was always difficult.

The box had stopped glowing. Beaky looked at it again, and saw the neat hand-written words on the side:

Press top to open

He pressed. The lid of the box flew open, like the lid of a Jack-in-the-box, but it wasn't a Jack that popped out, it was a puff of blue smoke.

The puff of smoke drifted round the table, took a look at the canary, and came floating back to a point just in front of Beaky's long nose, where it steadied itself in the air.

"You wished!" it said. "Only

two to go now!"

Beaky had never been spoken to by a puff of smoke before, but he took it well.

"Two? Two what?" he managed to say.

"Wishes!" said the puff, rather impatiently. "You wished, didn't you? That's one gone. Wasted, as

usual, if you ask me. But then *nobody* ever does ask me! I'm just a Genie, after all!"

"A Genie?" said Beaky.

"A Three Wish Genie, and you've had one," said the Genie.

Then they both heard Beaky's Mum coming down the stairs.

"Back in my box!" said the Genie, hurriedly, and back it went.

"Ready for school, Brian?" asked Mrs Kelly.

"Mum," said Beaky. "There was a . . ." He stopped. Then he picked up the red box, and slipped it into his pocket.

"Ready!" he said, and off he went.

Chapter Two

Beaky walked down the road to school, wondering what to do with his wishes.

He could turn his teacher, Mr McGrow, into an elephant or he could make everybody's trousers fall down or he could turn the school into a spaceship or he could shorten his nose, or he could do anything else he wanted to.

"Only three wishes!" the Genie warned. "That's my rule. You get three wishes, and after that you've had it!" Then the Genie added scornfully, "You'll make a fool of yourself, of course. They all do."

"What if I wish for *six* wishes?" Beaky asked, because he wasn't a Kelly for nothing. The Kellys were cunning.

"If you cheat, you lose the lot!" said the Genie, firmly.

"Who decides if I'm cheating?"

"I do," said the Genie.

"That isn't fair!" said Beaky.

"I make up the rules, and you

have to stick to them," said the Genie. "There aren't many Three Wish Genii around these days. You're lucky to have met me at all."

Then Beaky had to stop talking to the Genie, because he met Nellie Armstrong. Nellie was a big girl and a good fighter and a friend of Beaky's, but he didn't want her to know about his Genie. Beaky's Kelly cunning told him to keep his Genie top secret, until he had worked out what to do with the two wishes he had left.

Beaky and Nellie bumped into Archie Purvis and Bin Smith at the door of the classroom. Bin was the

3B poet, and he had just thought up another of his short poems.

"Beaky Kelly loves our Nellie!" Bin said, proudly.

"You shut up, Bin!" Nellie said.

"Knock your teeth in for you, Nellie Armstrong!" Archie Purvis said, cheerfully.

"You and what army?" said Nellie.

"Me and Bin," said Archie, trying to look tough, which was difficult, because he had knock knees and glasses. Nobody was allowed to hit Archie because of his glasses, and so Archie spent a lot of time threatening to fight people, and then if anyone hit him Archie

told Mr McGrow and Mr McGrow went wild.

"That's two to one!" said Nellie.

"One and a half to one!" said Beaky. "Archie only counts as a half."

"What sniffs and grows? Beaky's nose!" chanted Bin the poet.

Beaky looked hard at him. "I could turn you into a toad!" he said.

The exciting thing was that he could! He could turn Bin Smith into a worse toad than Bin already was, or a dachshund with little short legs. He had a good mind to do it, too. Beaky didn't like people teasing him about his nose.

"Beaky Kelly's very smelly!" shouted Bin.

"And he has a big fat belly!" said Archie, unexpectedly. Archie was very pleased with himself, because he didn't often think of poems.

"Beaky Kelly Smelly Belly!" said Bin, who wasn't going to ignore a challenge like that. "Beaky Kelly Smelly Bel . . ."

"*I wish you'd shut up!*" Beaky said, fiercely.

Bin did shut up, right in the middle of shouting "Belly". He got as far as "Bel", and then his bin lid snapped shut. He blinked, he gurgled, and he tried to open his mouth again, but couldn't.

"Hmmmm!" Bin said, wagging his head desperately.

"What's the matter, Bin?" asked Archie.

"Hmmmmmm!" said Bin. "Hmmmmmmm!" The last bit was louder than the beginning, and Bin sounded frightened.

"Have you swallowed something, Bin?" Archie asked.

"His tongue, probably," said Nellie.

Beaky was staring at Bin, aghast!

Two wishes left, and he'd wasted one! There was Bin going "Hmmmmmmmm" on and on and on! Perhaps it would wear off . . . but if the wish didn't wear off Beaky knew that he would have to use his third wish to get Bin talking again, which seemed like a terrible waste of a wish.

Chapter Three

The situation called for all the Kelly cunning that Beaky could manage, but he didn't get time to think about it, because at that moment Mr McGrow walked in.

"Good morning!" he said, and banged his books down on the desk. Then he turned and glared at the class, through his glasses. Mr McGrow had the worst temper in the whole of Maypole Street Primary. He was small, with a bristly moustache and bright red hair, and this morning he was crosser than ever. He had tripped over the cat when he was getting out of bed, and banged his head on the bed post.

"You may sit," he said.

He put the class register on his desk, and started reading out the names. When he said a name, the person had to say "Present" and then Mr McGrow put a tick on the register.

"Present!" said Nellie, when it

came to her turn, which was close to the beginning, of course. Mr McGrow worked his way down the register past Beaky and Archie Purvis and then he said "Smith?"

"Hhhhhhmmmmmmm!" said Bin.

"Present!" said Beaky, thinking quickly.

Mr McGrow looked up. "I'm sure Smith can speak for himself, Kelly!" he said, sternly. Beaky wasn't sure. In fact, Beaky knew that Bin couldn't speak for himself, unless you call saying "Hhhhhhmmmm" speaking.

"Smith?" said Mr McGrow.

"Hmmmmmmmmmmmhhh!"

"Smith! Stop that noise and answer me directly, boy!" thundered Mr McGrow.

"Hmmmmmmmmmmh!"

"Gross impertinence!" cried Mr

McGrow, and he got up from his desk and headed for Bin, who kept on "Hmmmmmmmh"ing, and by this time was looking very scared.

"Smith!" Mr McGrow stood right over Bin. "Answer me boy!"

Poor Bin's eyes were popping out of his head, and his chin was working, but he couldn't open his bin lid and he couldn't speak.

"SMITH!" roared Mr McGrow, grabbing poor little Bin by the shoulder and shaking him.

"*I wish you had a big monster picking on you!*" Beaky muttered and then . . . too late . . . he realised what he had done.

The third wish . . .

Right in front of the class, Mr McGrow shrunk, down and down, until he was just a speck on

the floor . . . and down there, on the floor, he met a big monster.

It was a beetle.

Chapter Four

"Hmmmmm! Hmmmmmmmmh! Hmmmmmmmmm!" said Bin Smith, excitedly. He was down on his hands and knees on the floor, looking for Mr McGrow.

Everyone else was looking as well.

They couldn't see him, but they could hear him.

Mr McGrow was being picked on by the beetle. The sound of his angry voice, which was now a high-pitched squeak, was coming from the floor beside Bin's desk.

The beetle had never had a dinner that shouted at it. It had never seen anything like Mr McGrow, who was dancing up and down and waving his tiny fists at it. The beetle ran away, but Mr McGrow kept on shouting.

"I can't see him, but I can *hear* him!" Nellie Armstrong said. "He sounds awfully cross."

"Hmmm! Hmmm! Hmmm!" said Bin, nodding in agreement.

"I don't understand what is

happening!" said Archie Purvis, nervously.

So Beaky told him.

"You're kidding!" said Archie, and everybody else.

"No I'm not!" Beaky insisted. "Why do you think Mr McGrow has shrunk, and Bin can only say 'Hhhhhhmmm!'?"

"There are no such things as Genii!" said Archie.

"There are no such things as tiny teachers, either," said Nellie. "But we've got one."

They all got down on the floor to look for Mr McGrow, and at last they found him. He was trying to climb to safety on Bin's school-bag, so that he wouldn't get trampled on by large feet. Everybody had been rushing around looking for tiny Mr McGrow, without being careful where they put their feet. It was very frightening for the tiny teacher.

"I've got him!" Nellie said. "But I can't make out what he is saying."

Perhaps it was just as well. Mr McGrow was dancing about on Nellie's hand shouting and bawling and threatening to do awful things if he didn't grow back to full size straight away.

"Get the dustpan, Archie!" Nellie said.

Archie got the dustpan from Mr McGrow's cupboard, and Nellie put Mr McGrow inside and closed the flap. It was dark and dusty inside the dustpan, and Mr McGrow got frightened and began to sneeze. Then he started to bounce up and down battering against the

side of the dustpan and shouting to be let out.

"Put him in the Lego house!" said Beaky, and Nellie did.

Mr McGrow fitted easily into the Lego house. He sat and sulked in the living room.

"What are we going to do?" Nellie asked.

Everybody looked at Beaky.

"I don't know," he said. "I've used all my three wishes!"

"Hmmmmmmmmmm!" said Bin. "Hmmmm! Hmmm!"

"I think," said Archie, carefully, "I think Bin's saying we should ask the Genie!"

Chapter Five

Beaky tapped the lid of the red box, and it flew open. The puff of smoke came out, and floated around the Lego house. Mr McGrow was looking out of the living room window. It took a look at Mr McGrow, then it flew over and had a look at Bin and then it puffed over and settled in the air, just in front of Beaky's nose.

"Made a mess of it, didn't you?" said the Genie. "I knew you would, stupid!"

"Y-e-s," admitted Beaky, who didn't like being called 'stupid', "But . . ."

"No buts!" said the Genie. "Stupid people always say 'but'!"

"But I haven't made my real wishes at all!" Beaky went on, stubbornly. "I wanted to win the football pools and have a short nose and . . ."

"You wished, and you got what you wished for," said the Genie, smugly. "You're all the same, you humans. Always get it wrong! I have a good laugh, sometimes. Stupid, stupid! That's what you are!"

"Beaky can't help being stupid," said Archie. "But the point is, will his wishes wear off, or will Bin go on saying 'Hmmmmmmh' and Mr McGrow have to live in our Lego house forever?"

"Take's a wish to fix a wish," said the Genie. "That's my rule. I make up the rules you know, and I always stick to them."

"I wish Bin could speak, and Mr McGrow would grow!" said Nellie, quickly.

The puff of smoke made a tiny startled circle in the air, like a smoke ring, and spun round.

"I don't recall granting *you* any wishes," it said. "Wishes made before they're personally granted by me simply don't count, I'm afraid. Those are my rules, and I'm sticking to them."

"What can we do?" asked Nellie.

"Oh, find another Genie, I suppose," said the Genie. "If you can!"

"Could you grant *me* three wishes?" Nellie asked.

"I *could*," said the Genie, "if you asked very politely."

"Please, Genie, would you be very very kind and grant me three wishes? Please? I'm sure you are a very good and kind and nice Genie really."

"No," said the Genie. "No I won't grant you three wishes and no I'm not good and kind and nice."

"You're rotten!" Nellie said.

"That's right!" said the Genie, and it gave itself another little smokey spin of pleasure. "I'm only a Three Wish Genie," the Genie went on. "Three wishes a day. That's my rule. Of course, you could ask me tomorrow, if I haven't moved on."

"Moved on!" said Archie in alarm. "But that would mean that

Bin and Mr McGrow would be like they are for ever!"

"No they won't!" said Beaky, who wasn't a cunning Kelly for nothing. "You granted me *three* wishes, didn't you?" he said to the Genie.

"Yes!" said the Genie. "You shrank your teacher and you lost that boy's voice and you wished for something to happen. I may be only a Three Wish a Day Genie, but you've got to admit that something did happen."

"You told Nellie that she couldn't make a wish *before* you'd granted her one!" said Beaky. "You said it wouldn't count!"

"Y-e-s," agreed the Genie, thoughtfully.

"But you didn't grant me three wishes until *after* I'd asked for something to happen!" said Beaky. "You said you always stuck to your rules. Well, that means I've only had two wishes, doesn't it?"

There was a long silence.

"I've got one wish left!" said Beaky triumphantly.

"Hmmmmmmmmmmh!" said Bin, and Mr McGrow started to squeak and jump about in the Lego house.

"*One* wish!" said the Genie, with an unpleasant laugh, "one wish, two problems!" The Genie spun around in the air in delight.

"You're going to have to leave one of them stuck like that forever!" said Nellie.

"No I'm not," said Beaky. "I wish . . . I wish that everything was back the way it was, before the Genie came!"

There was a whirry sound in the classroom, like a clockwork motor running down.

"What's that?" Nellie asked.

"Hmmmmmmh," said Bin.

There was a smell like something burning and then . . .

CRAAACKLEFFIILLLZZZ

Beaky was back in his own house.

He came down to breakfast, feeling bored. He ate his cornflakes, feeling bored, and then he started to pack his school-bag, feeling bored.

"I wish something would *happen*!" he said.

But nothing did.